9

Nine Nights

Your New Little Black Book For Personal Financial Empowerment

A date night action plan designed to help couples become actively-engaged partners in their family's financial affairs

9

Nine Nights

Your New Little Black Book For Personal Financial Empowerment

A date night action plan designed to help couples become actively-engaged partners in their family's financial affairs

Publishing, composition, and design managed by Niche Pressworks

www.nichepressworks.com

ISBN: 978-1533097347

Dedication

Although my parents, married for 60 years, have what most people consider a very traditional marriage, they have been a solid influence on my brothers and me with regard to how they handle their finances. From day one, they both knew all the details about their bank accounts, investments, mortgages, and every other aspect of their financial lives. My parents make all financial decisions together, after considerable thought, discussion and research. My brothers and I continue the tradition with our respective partners.

This book is dedicated to my parents, to my wonderful family, and to my clients, whose experiences inspired the writing of this book.

Acknowledgements

My clients: Thank you for supporting this effort and allowing me to use your stories to financially empower other people.

My "marketing guru," Nicole: Thank you for your enthusiasm, creativity and insight. You helped me turn what most people consider boring into a necessary, but entertaining, project.

Linda, Geoff, Todd, Jeff, Heidi and Kathie: Thank you for your thoughtful and honest edits and input, and for taking the time to review the book.

Jeff, Katie and Max: Thank you, dear family, for your support during this process. You three are the best!

Contents

Preface

Financial clarity brings a freedom and peace of mind that no amount of money could ever buy. Furthermore, when freedom is combined with responsibility, an economically independent woman can become a powerful force in the world.

Barbara Stanny, author of *Prince Charming Isn't Coming*

As a personal financial assistant, I worked for many years with well-heeled women and men – entrepreneurs, corporate executives, small business owners, doctors, and attorneys. People who inherited wealth and those who enjoyed creating and building wealth in their chosen careers. My clients included married couples, widows, divorcees, and single men and women of all backgrounds and experiences. During those years, I noticed each of my clients understood one very important concept - their financial life, and their personal financial literacy, needed to be protected, nurtured, and improved. With the assistance of individual "financial advisory teams" - power-packed groups consisting of estate attorneys, financial planners, accountants, insurance agents and investment advisors – my clients slowly and intentionally put into place thoughtful planning and a process of self-learning which allowed them to confidently manage their wealth.

None of these clients began their adult lives and careers with a solid knowledge of financial matters. As their wealth grew, however, they realized outside professional advice and a commitment to personal preparation and financial education can have a positive impact on the bottom line.

Financial planning, estate planning, and financial literacy are not only for wealthy people. Everyone, no matter the size of their checkbook or stock portfolio, no matter if they are just beginning their career or are nearing retirement, can benefit greatly by increasing their financial knowledge, participating in decisions with their own financial advisory team, and strategically planning for the future.

Women and Wealth

Women, now more than ever, have an obligation to themselves, their partners, their children, and their grandchildren to develop their financial acumen. **Seventy percent** (70%) of the wealth transferred over the next 40 years will be inherited by **women**.[2] Baby boomers and millennials will be the transferors and recipients of the largest intergenerational amount of wealth recorded to date.[2] Anyone who expects to receive or leave an inheritance must begin or continue learning how to manage this important responsibility.

Today, approximately 50% of estates in the United States valued over $5 million are controlled by **women**.[2] More importantly, by the year 2030, 66% of the total private wealth in the United States will be held by **women**.[2]

For financial advisors everywhere, this is a clarion call to include and advise women on an equal par with men, whether they are spouses, divorcees, or single.

At least one of the "Three D's" (Death, Disability, and Divorce) will impact all of us; unfortunately many must deal with each of them. No one should be caught ill-equipped, financially, in the event of these life-changing events. Prepare your estate planning and medical documents *now*. Be ready when your family is impacted by the death or disability of your partner or if a divorce is a future possibility.

Another important statistic to note: **the average age of widowhood in the United States is 56**.[1] The time will come in every woman's life when she will be single (whether she is widowed, separated or divorced, or never married). She will have no choice but to accept the task of managing her financial affairs for the next 20 to 40 years.

Don't wait until you are ready to take action. Instead, take action to be ready.

Jensen Siaw, Motivational Speaker

This is a Journey. Embrace the Process.

The previous section was intended as a call to action for my women readers, but I wrote this book to encourage *both* women and men to take the first step in thinking about and developing an action plan *before* facing an emergency, a death in your family, or before you give yourself one more reason to delay strengthening your financial preparedness.

The Introduction and subsequent chapters in this book guide you through the process of improving your financial literacy, assist you in developing a handy file of essential documents to keep at your fingertips in the event of a family emergency, and, most importantly, increase your confidence when dealing with financial matters.

I encourage you to embrace the subject matter, make it fun, and reward yourself when you've accomplished the assignments detailed in each chapter.

You can do this!

Introduction

Knowing about the assets, helping to keep the records, helping to make the decisions are all part of the economic partnership modern marriage is supposed to be.

Shelby White, author of
What Every Woman Should Know About Her Husband's Money

In the United States, the responsibility for all things related to family finances has typically been shouldered by the husband. In far too many cases, the wife has not participated in the family's financial life, whether due to her preference or her husband's. Unfortunately, if the husband dies or becomes incapacitated, the unprepared wife is left to deal with not only her husband's death or illness, but also the confusion, stress, and misunderstanding that often result when overseeing the family's financial affairs for the first time.

We have heard the argument women should more actively participate with their partners in the day-to-day management of family financial matters. Initiating this effort, however, can sometimes be a bit difficult or even awkward for partners. Even so, I encourage commitment to this important project. Increasing the comfort level of both partners in all things financial benefits the entire family. Here are some thoughts on how to begin the process.

My first suggestion is to have partners examine together their respective roles in managing the family's finances. Communication is key. Listen closely to what each of you has to say about financial matters. Work constantly toward a pattern of ongoing discussion without fear of negative feedback.

Next, develop a habit of studying and sharing the latest news about financial topics. The Internet, books, newspaper and magazine articles, and television business programs all are great resources of financial terms, trends, basic information, tips and strategies.

Communication and ongoing research are strategies a successful Chief Financial Officer (CFO) uses in the business world, as well as budgeting, cash flow analysis, and strategic planning for the future. Why not manage your family's finances the same way and define yourselves as Co-CFOs of your family's financial matters? As Co-CFOs, partners can work together on three main areas: focus on research and discovery (**Study**); share the duties (**Participate**); and anticipate the future (**Prepare**).

Study: Learning financial terminology, becoming savvy in the use of financial tools appropriate for your situation, and keeping up to date on those tools and strategies not only empower you to become comfortable with financial matters, but allow you to embrace this vital aspect of your lives.

Throughout this book, financial terms discussed are in ***bold and italics.*** The Glossary provides a list of these terms and their definitions.

Think about ways to make this process interesting, fun, and a great way to deepen your relationship with your partner. Here are a few ideas.

- ☑ Have discussions with your friends or family members about general financial topics.

- ☑ Select two books on financial topics. Refer to the Bibliography at the end of this book for some very good options. Each of you reads one of the books and shares the highlights with the other, giving you the advantage of gaining information from two books while reading only one.

- ☑ Have honest conversations with each other about your feelings toward finances, your preferred methods of dealing with finances, and how this affects your partner. Discuss how the current system works and if it is the best way for the two of you to manage your financial lives.

☑ Learn financial terminology. As a starting point for your study, most of the terms contained in the Glossary in the back of this book are discussed, at least briefly, in the chapters and are relevant for readers in just about every facet of life.

☑ Read online articles or blogs, newspapers, and books about finances. Your local library and online book sites have a good collection to peruse. If you are in a book club, add a financial strategies book to your reading selections (refer to the Bibliography at the back of this book).

Participate: Be an active participant in your financial life! Cary Siegel, author of *Why Didn't They Teach Me This In School?*,[3] talks about marrying (and staying married to) the "financially right" person. In this book, he encourages ongoing and frequent discussions about financial matters with your partner, and states, "If you do this, you'll be setting yourself up not only for financial success but also for an open, honest marriage." What a great reason to work on your financial literacy skills!

As Co-CFOs, jointly attend meetings with members of your financial team. Refine your list of topics and questions and read up on the latest data and trends in advance so you can comfortably discuss these ideas with each other and with advisors. During the meetings, share with your partner the task of asking questions or introducing discussion topics. Take notes during the meetings. The notes do not need to be detailed, but a few words to remind you both of items for follow-up is helpful. Ask the advisor to send you an email or letter detailing the meeting and be sure to take action on the items assigned to you.

Periodically change financial duties with one another. Scott Holsapple of the Mutual Fund Store suggests partners switch roles "so they know finances from all directions. If one is paying bills and the other is meeting with the financial adviser, change those roles so you get the exposure."[4]

Prepare: Review or develop and put into place estate planning documents and medical directives. Name *guardians* for your minor children. Strategize together your future financial goals and plans. Common goals, planned with input and enthusiasm from both partners, will surely be more successful than a plan generated by one without ideas or agreement from the other.

Most importantly, gather all your financial, medical, business, and personal data into a handy organization file folder. Review and keep these documents updated at least annually.

The more you **Study, Participate, and Prepare,** the more confident you become stepping into the role of Co-CFOs. And, you set a wonderful example for your children, siblings, parents and friends, which may put them on a path to confidently manage their own financial lives.

> *We were not taught financial literacy in school. It takes a lot of work and time to change your thinking and to become financially literate.*

> **Robert Kiyosaki**, Financial Author

The Bottom Line:
Take an active, dynamic role in
your financial future!

Your Nine Nights to Financial Empowerment

As a professional organizer and personal financial assistant, I help clients with budgeting, bill paying, project management, and home and office organization. I offer my experience and knowledge to you in book form, but it is the same information I share with my clients.

I am available on a short-term basis to help you and your partner with organization. My website, www.organizedsolutionsllc.net, provides more information on my one-day "Get Us Organized!" sessions.

My goal is for everyone to be financially organized and financially empowered. Let's work together to make this interesting for both you and your partner. No financial advice is offered in this book – that is the job of your financial team. I offer strategies to help you feel more comfortable embracing finances, terminology, and organization to prepare you for the future.

The Plan

This book is organized and designed so information and tasks can be worked on together with your partner over the course of nine date nights. Each date night focuses on a different segment of financial literacy, organization or both. Arrange for quiet times together with few distractions. If you have young children, put them to bed early. Silence your phones and turn off email and social media distractions.

If you are single, enlist older children, trusted friends or siblings to assist you. Schedule nine "Girls' Nights," or plan a weekend with your best friends to complete the assignments. Not only will you have a supportive circle of friends and family to help you with this journey, but they can benefit themselves from working with you. Of course, as a single person your role is not a Co-CFO but a *Sole*-CFO, and your responsibility and commitment to keep an eye on your financial life is even more important.

I will ask you to locate documents to study and copy, so you will need access each date night to a printer/copier. The copied documents will be placed into an accordion-type file folder; keep the file close at hand during these date nights. Some readers may want a scanned version of the documents as well. If your printer/copier has a scan feature, all the better. Consider keeping a notebook of ideas, terms and projects the two of you want to work on during these nine date nights.

To keep your important documents easy to access, I recommend purchasing two accordion-type file folders with 12-13 tabbed pockets and a secure flap cover. The file folders you choose should fit handily in a safe deposit box or a locked, and preferably fireproof, file drawer. Appendix B provides a list of options for an organization folder. One file folder will be used to house all your original documents, and should be stored securely in a safe deposit box or locked file drawer. In the second folder, you will keep copies of these documents. This is the mobile file you can pack and take with you anywhere. Store it in a safe place in your home for quick access. Once you have purchased the file folders, develop seven tab headings for each:

FINANCIAL	TRAVEL
ESTATE PLANNING & RETIREMENT	BUSINESS
MEDICAL	OTHER
CONTACTS	

These tab headings correspond with date-night chapters in the book, so having the tab headings prepared and ready ahead of your date nights will be beneficial.

If you opt not to follow the nine night program, the organization aspect of this book – developing all the documents you need for your accordion file – can be done in much less time. Schedule one or two days of locating and copying documents, and you will have a completed file. You can then read financial articles, blogs or books to boost your financial literacy.

The Reluctant Partner

I understand you may have a partner who is not necessarily receptive to participating in this effort. Not everyone is ready or willing to share this responsibility, although doing so would benefit you both, now and into the future. Here are some suggestions to let you proceed on your own:

☑ Schedule just one or two date nights together. Focus those date nights on the first and the fifth chapters of the book, as they contain topics requiring input from both of you. You can handle the balance of the book by yourself or with the assistance of a trusted friend or adult children.

☑ Work on one of the chapters on your own, then show your results to your partner to encourage feedback and comments. This may encourage your partner to consider participating with you in the project.

☑ Imagine your partner is incapacitated and you have to do the work and research on your own. What can you learn now to offset problems in a real-life crisis?

If all else fails, ask your reluctant family Co-CFO to read the next page, which is an open letter of encouragement to share the family CFO duties with you.

An Open Letter to the
Primary CFO of Your Family

Dear Family CFO:

After years of hard work and dedication creating a legacy for you and for your family, taking time now to work with your partner as co-CFOs ensures your partner, your children, and your grandchildren will be able to enjoy all you have built.

Handing over financial responsibility upon your death or disability to someone who is unprepared, uninformed, and unadvised is not in the best interest of your family. Even if you have consulted with advisors, developed your estate plan with great thought and consideration, and are satisfied with the results, if the plan is not discussed and shared with your partner – typically the primary beneficiary of all you've worked to achieve – the planning and consideration may be for naught.

Anything can happen overnight – and usually does. Did you know the average age for a woman to become widowed is 56?[1] Preparing now for a family emergency situation, where one of you becomes incapacitated or passes away, will be a tremendous gift to you both. *This is the most loving gesture you can make to your family.*

If you are well-organized, it will be easy to share with your partner your papers to reassure plans are in place. Discussing the current plans also allows you to realize some missing elements you can work together to complete.

I hope you will take these words to heart. Include your partner in your financial planning and day-to-day financial affairs, and you both will be the richer for it – *both literally and figuratively.*

Best regards,
Laurie Teal

The First Date Night

Your Go-Forward Financial Strategy Plan

You have to be the masters of your own financial future.

Suze Orman, Financial Author

What you'll create tonight:

A go-forward plan laying out roles for each of you regarding your financial life.

What you'll need:

This book, a notepad and pen for note taking, possibly a computer.

Welcome to the first date night! I am excited you are taking on this project and are interested in improving your financial savviness.

Look into each other's eyes. Commit to this project for your mutual benefit. Take a few deep breaths. Let's begin!

Get comfortable together on the sofa, or talk while preparing a delicious meal for two. This is your opportunity to have a deep, meaningful discussion about your financial lives.

Which of you does what? Who pays the bills? Is one of you the main point of contact with your accountant, your stock broker, your attorney, your financial advisor? Is the current way of doing things the best use of your respective skill sets and interests?

Who takes the lead in making financial decisions for the two of you? Why? Is this the best method? What if the other wants to be more involved? How would that play out in terms of communication, research, and general learning? How would you develop strategies so the two of you can serve as Co-CFOs?

Who are the outside advisors your family uses as its financial support team? Share this information with one another, and discuss each advisor's role in the financial team. Develop a quick list of these advisors, along with their contact information.

Does the other partner want to be more involved with these outside advisors? If so, how can you change the process so you both have an opportunity to communicate and work with your financial team?

If you decide one of you will continue to take the lead on communications, this does not exonerate the other from responsibility and knowledge. *Both* of you need to dive in and share financial responsibilities.

> *I don't think business news is just for old white men with money.*
>
> **Neil Cavuto**, Business Television Anchor and Commentator

As painful as it may be for many people, learning financial terminology, becoming savvy in the use of financial tools appropriate for your situation, and keeping up to date on those tools and strategies will not only empower you to become comfortable with financial matters, but allow you to confidently embrace this aspect of your life. A few ideas to get you started are listed below.

☑ As discussed in the Introduction, select two books or articles on financial topics. (Several very good books are listed in the Bibliography at the end of this book.) Each of you reads one of the books, and shares the highlights with the other. This gives you the advantage of gaining information from two books while reading only one.

☑ If either of you is in a book group, add a financial strategies book to your reading selections (refer to the Bibliography at the back of this book). Invite the partners of your book group to participate so all of you can discuss the topics.

☑ Is one of you an intrepid researcher on the Internet? Does one of you love to read or watch business television shows? Do you enjoy talking with friends about the latest in finances? If so, share this knowledge with your partner.

☑ Refer to the Glossary at the end of this book for basic financial terminology and definitions.

☑ Enjoy game nights with family or friends. The classic Monopoly™, Payday™ and The Game of Life™ are still great tools to teach and review personal financial topics. www.moneycrashers.com provides a list of five recommended board games about money.

☑ Research the Internet for more ideas for the entire family to become involved in learning about personal finance. The Bibliography at the end of this book also lists some websites for your consideration. Teaching others is a great way to learn more about various topics.

☑ InvestorWords.com is a website with a "financial word of the day" you can receive via email – it's free!

Results. By the end of this evening, the two of you should have:

☑ Laid out a plan of action, refine what you are currently doing, or commit to the status quo in terms of what each of you has responsibility for in your financial lives.

☑ Identified the names and contact information for each of your financial team advisors – insurance agent, accountant, estate planning attorney, financial advisor, investment advisor, etc. Keep a copy of this list; you will add it to the Contacts tab in your organization file (discussed in Chapter 6).

☑ Selected at least one book or article for each of you to read.

Congratulations on your first night of work!

The Second Date Night

Your Organization Strategy

Organizing is something you do before you do something, so that when you do it, it is not all mixed up.

A.A. Milne

One of my clients has a husband who has been travelling internationally for years. He recently suffered a series of health issues, but continues his business and the associated travel. My client recently decided it would be prudent for her to maintain an emergency documents file. We purchased an accordion file, into which she placed copies of every important document she would need in the event her husband has an emergency out of the country and she must jump on the next plane to be with him. She keeps the file in a safe and accessible place in her home, and we update it at least twice a year.

What You'll Create Tonight:

Completion of the Financial tab of your organization file folders.

What You'll Need:

This book, your two organization file folders, a copier/scanner, a notebook and pen or your computer, access to financial documents (such as credit cards, vehicle titles, insurance policies, checking/saving accounts, etc.).

*W*elcome to your second date night! This night speaks to the Organizer part of your Co-CFO roles.

Caring for Your Important Documents

I mentioned in the Introduction the development and use of an emergency documents file. This will be a great tool to have ready should your family face an emergency and you or your partner need quick access to vital documents.

Purchase two sturdy accordion files with 12-13 tabbed pockets and a flap cover for security. Appendix B provides a list of sources for organization files. One of the accordion files will house copies of all these original documents, and will be your handy emergency documents file you can access and update on a regular basis.

You will be locating and reviewing **the most important documents of your life** for this project. Once you have the original documents in hand, it is vital for you to properly protect – and easily locate – these papers going forward. Place all the original documents into the second accordion folder and store the folder in a safe deposit box or locked, secure, and fireproof (if possible) home safe or file drawer. Accessing the documents later will be much easier if they are stored in one location. Your estate attorney can retain a copy of your wills and other estate planning documents in the event you do not have access to a secure file or safe deposit box. A quick call to the attorney to provide a copy of the documents is all you need if you wish to review the information or in the event of an emergency.

If you use a safe deposit box to house these documents, be sure both you and your partner are authorized to access the box. In the event of death or incapacitation of one of you, the bank may delay access to the contents if you are not dually authorized.

Thanks to my client's idea in the story at the beginning of this chapter, I have helped several others prepare an organization file. They all agree it is a great resource. The file's portability allows them to easily access both the folder and the contents in an emergency. An annual or semi-annual review of the contents is required to keep the file updated.

Paper vs. Digital

I have friends who have scanned all their important documents into a folder on their computer or to a USB drive. Many people don't like handling a lot of paper, and prefer having all documentation stored electronically. I understand the preference, but argue for a paper file for these reasons:

1. Not everyone uses a laptop computer, and if you happen to be out of town (or out of the country) and need to quickly retrieve the documents, accessibility would be difficult and time-consuming.

2. If you use a laptop and carry it with you everywhere, access to the documents is available. (Please be sure to password-protect and encrypt the folder containing these documents.) However, many groups needing the documentation (such as hospitals) require paper copies of documents. An electronic copy often will not suffice. (Two good examples of original or *certified* documents needed are death certificates and DD Form 214, the official discharge document for the military.)

If you prefer to store your documents electronically, I offer a few suggestions. First, back up the scanned documents to a secure USB drive and password-protect the file. Store the USB drive in a safe place, such as a safe deposit box, safe, or locked filing cabinet. Second, be sure someone else (your partner, a trusted friend or family member) knows the password so the file can be accessed should you be unable to do so.

There are several cloud-based document storage options to consider. Appendix B provides some websites for you to research and compare.

Get to Know Your Copier and Scanner

Tonight you will dig in your filing cabinets, drawers, wallets, and wherever you keep your financial information. You will make copies or scans – and lots of them! You will place these into the Financial tab of your organization file for quick access and reference.

You may want to divide the task. One of you can operate the copier/scanner while the other sorts the documents to be copied or scanned. Other date nights will involve making copies or scans of additional documents and paperwork, so consider switching the task next time.

Include the following in your organization files:

- ☑ Copies of all your credit and debit cards (back and front). Include retail store account cards as well as major credit cards.

- ☑ A list of your checking and savings accounts (including those of your children), account numbers, and the contact information for the financial institution(s).

- ☑ A listing of *assets*, owned jointly or separately. This includes investments, retirement or pension accounts, real estate, vehicles, jewelry, art and other collectibles.

- ☑ If you have made a list of the contents of your home, whether in print or on video, add to the organization file a note as to the location of the list or video for quick reference.

- ☑ Copies of vehicle titles, such as auto, boat, motorcycle, and RV. Review these titles to check who is listed as the owner of the vehicle.

Note: If only you or your partner is listed as the owner, the vehicle is *not* jointly owned.

One More Note: The original titles should always be stored in a safe place, such as a safe deposit box, locked and preferably fireproofed filing cabinet, etc.

- ☑ Copies of vehicle loans - auto, boat, motorcycle, or RV. Include account numbers and contact information.

☑ Copies of the *Declarations Pages* of homeowners or renters insurance policies, auto insurance policies, *umbrella* coverage policies, additional insured policies (fine arts, computers, etc.). While you are making copies, spend some time reviewing the policies to ensure coverage is up to date and sufficient for your needs. If you have recently made a large purchase, such as a computer, television, or a piece of art, a call to your insurance agent is in order to be sure the item is sufficiently insured.

☑ A copy of deeds or mortgage/lease information on your home(s) or apartment. Again, include the account number, as well as the contact information for the mortgage company or apartment leasing office.

☑ A copy of any other loan documents, including student loans. Please include on the copy the contact information for your quick reference.

☑ *Certified* copies of birth certificates, marriage license, divorce decree, or death certificate if your spouse has died. If you are remarried, you should keep a copy of the license from the first marriage as well as the divorce decree in the file folders.

☑ Copies of your Social Security cards.

☑ A copy of your *prenuptial agreement*, if you have one.

☑ A copy of your divorce decree, if you were previously divorced.

☑ A listing of the contents of your safe or safe deposit box. Also, a note as to the location of your safe or safe deposit box key/passcode, and a list of the owner(s) and authorized users. As discussed earlier in this chapter, if only one of you is listed as the authorized user for the box, the other may not be quickly granted access in the event of the authorized user's death. Consider a visit to the bank to include your partner as an authorized user. If you rent a safe deposit box at a bank, include the address and phone number of the bank branch.

☑ Copies of *disability* and/or *long-term care insurance policies*. A copy of the *Declarations Page* will be sufficient for these files. The Declarations Page is the one-page overview of your coverage, and includes the amount of your insurance, the annual premium, the owner of the policy, etc. Store original policies in a safe deposit box or locked filing cabinet.

Results: By the end of this evening, the two of you should have:

☑ All the documents copied and placed into the Financial tab of your organization files. Store original documents in the second file you purchased.

☑ Noted any changes you need to make to homeowners, auto, or umbrella insurance policies.

☑ If some of these documents were not available this evening, locate them as soon as possible so they can be copied and added to your organization file.

Nice job! Reward yourselves for your ongoing efforts.

The Third Date Night

Your Estate Planning Documents Strategy

Financial literacy is just as important in life as the other basics.

John W. Rogers, Jr., Founder of Ariel Investments

One of my clients left all the financial/estate/tax planning matters to her husband in order to focus on enjoying her retirement, her family, and her community interests. A few years ago she lost her husband very suddenly and most tragically, leaving her to deal with complicated estate planning issues. Fortunately, she was able to rely on competent, knowledgeable advisors who had long-term relationships with her husband and family to help streamline the process. However, she was enveloped for many months sorting through estate matters, learning along the way while still grieving the loss of her husband.

What You'll Create Tonight:

A plan to create, review, and possibly revise your estate planning documents.

What You'll Need:

This book, notebook and pen, estate planning documents you currently have.

*W*elcome to the third date night! Take another deep breath, because this date night will be fairly intense and finance-driven. Work together, be patient, and you'll get through the information in no time.

What is Estate Planning?

A person's estate consists of everything they own, whether it is a car, a savings account, a prized piece of art, or his/her retirement plan. Developing an estate plan ensures that, upon death, all assets owned by the person go to the people or groups specifically named to receive them. If properly developed and written, the estate planning documents help reduce taxes, court costs, and legal fees realized at death.

Three things every person's estate plan should include are:

1. An updated, signed *Will.*

2. A *Revocable* or *Irrevocable Trust.*

3. An *Advance Directive* and a *Durable Power of Attorney* document (these are discussed in detail in Chapter 5).

At minimum, the two of you should have signed, updated wills in place. This is especially true if you have assets to specifically *bequest* to others upon your death. Even if you feel you have few to no assets to pass on to heirs, having a current, valid will in place assists those left behind after your death. If you have wills, locate and review them together. If it has been some years since you developed your wills, this is a good opportunity to see if any changes or revisions are needed. It is generally recommended to review your wills at least every five years.

Questions to ask yourselves: Have you added to your family since the will was made? Have any of the *primary* or *contingent beneficiaries* listed in your will died or moved out of your life? Have any of the assets you planned to bequest been sold or gifted to others? Do you have other assets, acquired since the will was developed, you wish to bequest?

A *codicil* can be written as an attachment to the will to update the information, or the will can be completely rewritten to reflect your wishes. Your estate attorney is the point person on revising or rewriting wills.

A simple practice often overlooked is to periodically (every five years or so) review all beneficiaries named for various assets. People often neglect to check or update the beneficiaries for these accounts:

☑ Life insurance policies   ☑ Pensions

☑ Checking, savings, credit union   ☑ Investments

☑ 401(k) or 403(b)   ☑ IRAs

These assets are part of your estate as much as your home is. Take some time to review the beneficiaries currently listed to see if any changes need to be made. If you cannot locate the beneficiaries for these assets, contact your insurance agent, investment advisor, employer, pension or retirement account firm to request a copy of the current beneficiaries on these accounts.

> A financial planner acquaintance of mine told me about one of her clients, married many years to an older man who was divorced with children. She never questioned him about his estate plans. The man passed away, never changing the beneficiary designations for his home, investments, or other property. His first wife and children, who were still the beneficiaries, forced the client out of her home of 20 years and retained all the assets. The client had nothing to show for her marriage, even the home she lived in.

A review of any *revocable* or *irrevocable trusts* you have in place may prompt you to meet with your financial advisor or estate attorney if any changes are needed, especially if it has been more than five years since the trust documents were written. Does the language meet your current needs? Have you recently moved to another state? If so, the documents should be reviewed by an estate attorney to be sure they reflect the laws of the state in which you currently live. Is the *executor* or *executrix* named in the documents still the person you wish to handle your estate? Again, your estate attorney can help with developing a trust document or revising the one you currently have.

Guardians for Your Children

If you have minor children (under 18 years of age), have you named a *guardian* for them? In the event both of you die while you still have minor children, formally naming a trusted person or persons to care for your children is a tremendous gift not only for your children, but for your peace of mind.

It is generally suggested the person or persons you name to care for your children should not be the *executor/ executrix* of your wills and estates. The guardian, of course, should be able to work closely with the executor/executrix. But putting both of those responsibilities onto one person, even if the person is well qualified and capable, may not be in the best interest of your children or the assets you leave behind.

How to Pick the Perfect Advisor

Your financial advisory team, which typically consists of an accountant, financial or investment advisor, estate attorney, and an insurance agent, have specific roles to play in keeping your family on-track financially. Getting to know and trust these valued advisors helps you and your partner when planning your short- and long-term financial goals. Use their knowledge, experience, and resources to keep your financial strategy current and appropriate for your needs.

> One of my clients and her husband used an advisor for many years to manage their investments. While the husband was satisfied with their investment returns and the advisor's strategies, my client was beginning to feel the advisor was less-focused on their specific account. A few years ago, she and her husband switched to another investment advisor. When my client called to inform the original advisor, he inadvertently blurted out she was taking away his highest-commission investment account! My client and her husband are happily and closely working with the new advisor, who prides herself on transparency and full disclosure.

If you happen to be in the market for a financial planner, stockbroker, accountant, or estate attorney, I recommend several steps. First, research the advisors in your area. If you are looking for a financial advisor, ask your accountant or attorney for recommendations. Ask trusted friends or colleagues about their experiences with advisors. The Financial Industry Regulatory Authority, or FINRA, has an online website, http://brokercheck.finra.org, where anyone can view information about an investment advisor or broker – current certifications and licenses, any violations, complaints, or regulatory actions placed on the investment advisor or broker or the advisor's or broker's firm.

Once you have 3-5 firms on your short list, arrange an introductory meeting with each. Develop questions pertinent to your own situation to ask how they might handle your financial affairs. These questions are also applicable if you have advisors in place but have never asked them:

- ☑ How long has the advisor been in this business, and how many years has she/he worked for this firm?

- ☑ What are the advisor's qualifications? Is the advisor a *Certified Financial Planner*®, *Chartered Life Underwriter*, or other designation? Is the advisor up to date with continuing education programs and required registrations?

- ☑ What percentage of the advisor's clients are women? This question is particularly relevant if the two of you decide the female partner is the primary contact with the advisor.

- ☑ What is the firm's philosophy on investments, and what is the advisor's area of strength in terms of investments? How would this work with your financial situation and objectives?

- ☑ Ask for at least three references – from the advisor's current clients and other service professionals (attorneys, insurance agents, accounting firms, etc.) which work with the advisor and the advisor's firm.

- ☑ What is the fee structure and how are the fees charged? Financial advisors can charge fees in several different ways. Some charge commission on the investments they handle for clients. Others charge a percentage of their clients' investment holdings. And others charge a flat fee for their services, an hourly rate for financial advice, or a combination of all of the above.

☑ Would we have a signed written contract? What restrictions are in place if we wish to terminate services?

☑ Of course, the advisors should ask you questions as well. Here are some to consider:

☑ What are your ages and marital status?

☑ What are your *assets, liabilities*, annual income, *net worth*, monthly expenses (*fixed and variable*)? Do you have a current *personal financial statement* you can provide the advisor?

☑ What type of retirement account(s) do you have? How much do you have invested in your retirement account(s)?

☑ Do you have a *prenuptial agreement* in place?

☑ What insurance do you carry? This includes homeowners/ renters, auto, umbrella, health, life, disability, and long-term care insurance.

☑ Do you own a business? Do you jointly own the business, or are there one or more outside owners? Is there a *business continuation plan* in place? What insurance policies do you carry for your business?

☑ Will either of you inherit money one day?

☑ What is your philosophy on investments? Are you conservative or willing to tolerate *risk*? What are your thoughts about investing in *stocks, mutual funds, bonds, hedge funds*?

☑ How much money management are you comfortable handling on your own?

☑ Do you own a second home? Do you have a mortgage on this home, or is it owned outright?

☑ Are any major purchases being planned?

☑ Do you have dependents? If so, what are their ages? Is there a disabled dependent or one in school?

☑ Are there college costs in the future for you or your dependents?

☑ Are child support payments made or received?

☑ Have you thought about how long you plan to work until you retire?

☑ If you and/or your partner are 5-10 years away from retirement, have you considered your lives post-retirement and what *cash flow* needs you will have?

☑ What do you need the advisor to help you with, and what are you comfortable handling on your own?

Kerry Hannon, author of *Suddenly Single: Money Skills for Divorcees and Widows*,[5] provides some additional great questions to ask when interviewing financial or investment advisors, whether you are married or single.

Then, turn to trusted friends, co-workers, and family to ask about these advisors: Do they have a good reputation in the community? Are their clients happy? Are the clients' investments making money? What are their investment minimums and fees in relation to comparable advisors?

During the introductory meeting, try to determine this important point: **Do they respect their female clients and work with them as equals?** I stress this because if the two of you are working as a team in your financial lives and the advisor seems to speak only to your husband, the advisor may not feel comfortable with women or does not think you are equal team members. If either of you has concerns with the advisor, seek out another one.

Don't be afraid to ask your advisors questions. After all, it's *your* money and *your* future financial stability at stake.

After you have chosen an advisor, schedule at least three face-to-face meetings during the first year. This will give you and the advisor the opportunity to get to know one another, get a feel for each side's style, and put you in a better comfort level working with the new advisor. Meeting once or twice in subsequent years should be sufficient to keep the relationship strong. However, should you have any questions or concerns, don't wait for the next scheduled meeting. Phone or email your questions or concerns to your advisor as they come up. This helps them understand you better, and gives them a great opportunity to stay in touch.

Results: By the end of this evening, the two of you should have:

☑ Developed a list of your current estate planning documents.

☑ Developed a list of estate planning documents you need to create or revise.

☑ Decided which of you will contact your estate attorney to arrange for the creation/revision of the necessary documents.

☑ Checked to see all beneficiaries currently listed for your wills, life insurance policies, IRAs, investment accounts, pension accounts, etc. are up to date.

If you are in the market for a new advisor:

☑ Made a plan to contact trusted friends to ask for referrals. Split the list; each of you can make calls and share the results with each other.

☑ Researched advisors in your area, and scheduled appointments with 3-5 firms.

☑ Developed a set of questions for the initial interview meeting.

Three nights down. You're doing great!

The Fourth Date Night

Your Estate Planning Documents Strategy - Revisited

The number one problem in today's generation and economy is the lack of financial literacy.

Alan Greenspan, Former Chairman of the Federal Reserve

What You'll Create Tonight:

Completion of the Estate Planning and Retirement tab of your organization files.

What You'll Need:

This book, your organization files, a copier/scanner, estate planning documents, pension and retirement documents, life insurance declarations pages.

*W*elcome back! I hope the two of you have been doing a little light reading of financial articles or books on personal finance. Are you beginning to feel more financially empowered? We are working toward a good comfort level for you when dealing with financial matters. Keep up the effort – I am confident both of you will find it beneficial.

> A woman I know holds a weekly coffee at her home. Those Friday mornings offer a moveable feast of friends, friends of friends, and family members from all walks of life. Discussion topics range from family histories to current local events to the national economy. Keeping up with local and national news in all forms is mandatory to participate in the discussions. It has created new and lasting friendships for many of the attendees. I offer this idea to you as another way to continue your financial literacy education.

Tonight you will make copies of current financial and estate planning documents. Fire up your copier/scanner and open your files to retrieve your estate planning documents (discussed in detail in Chapter 3). Please copy the following documents and add them to the Estate Planning and Retirement tab in your organization files.

- ☑ Copies (*not* originals) of your most recent *wills*. If you did not review your current wills during the third Date Night, this is a great time to be sure they reflect your wishes. As discussed previously: if you purchased two accordion files, use the second file for all your original documents. House the file in a secure location.

- ☑ Copies (*not* originals) of your *revocable* or *irrevocable trusts*. Again, if you were not able to review the language of your current trust documents during the third Date Night, take the time to do this now. Be sure they are in line with your current wishes.

- ☑ Copies (*not* originals) of the *advance directives* for you and for your partner. Again, originals should be kept in a secure place. Advance directives are discussed in detail in Chapter 5.

- ☑ A copy of your pension and retirement documents, such as the current statements for your *IRAs*, *401(k)* or *403(b)* plans. Include contact information in case you need to make a quick call to these companies with questions.

☑ A copy of all *life insurance* policies, along with the contact information for your insurance agency. The ***Declarations Page*** is sufficient for your organization file. Review the Declarations Page to remind yourself of the amount of insurance you have purchased. If it has been some time (five years or more) since you have met with your life insurance agent, or if you have added dependents (natural or adopted children, for example), a review of your life insurance coverage may be in order. If you have taken out life insurance policies on your children, include in your organization files the Declarations Pages for these policies. As discussed in the third chapter, ensure the beneficiaries of your and your children's policies are up to date.

☑ A written list or note of any investment accounts you have, along with the account number(s) and contact information for the advisor.

Results: By the end of this evening, the two of you should have:

☑ All the documents copied and placed into the Estate Planning and Retirement tab of your organization files.

☑ Noted and taken action on any necessary changes to the beneficiaries of various assets.

☑ Noted if some documents were not readily available. Locate them as soon as possible so they can be copied and added to your organization file.

Congratulations! You are four nights closer to financial empowerment and claiming your titles as Co-CFOs.

The Fifth Date Night

Your Medical Emergency Strategy

Be prepared.

What You'll Create Tonight:

A plan to create, review, and possibly revise your medical emergency documents, including a medical history for each family member. Completion of the Medical tab of your organization files.

What You'll Need:

This book, your organization files, a copier/scanner, medical care plan documents, medical insurance cards, military papers if applicable.

*W*elcome to your fifth date night. One of your assignments tonight is to have another honest and candid conversation with each other.

Imagine one of you becomes incapacitated in some manner for an extended period of time. What that might look like, and how would it feel for each of you in such a situation? As the "able" partner, your time and energy resources would be strained…as the "recovering partner," your energy would be focused on rest and recovery, not on financial concerns. Fortunately, tonight's date will help you have this important portion of your affairs already well prepared.

> *Too often, the most intense education of your life begins at a time when you are in a state of emotional distress.*
>
> **Kerry Hannon**, Author of *Suddenly Single:*
> *Money Skills for Divorcees and Widows*

Medical Emergency Care Plan Documents

In Chapter 3, we discussed three documents that should be part of *every* family's estate plan. Let's carry that idea to this chapter, and discuss how these three documents should be part of *every* family's medical emergency care plan.

1. *Advance Directives* (also known as *Living Wills*)

2. *Durable Health Care Power of Attorney* documents

3. *Revocable Living Trust*

An *Advance Directive*, or *Living Will*, spells out your preferences for medical care, including whether you choose to receive medical care; pain relief methods; end-of-life directions on providing or withholding nutrition and resuscitation; and your preferences on organ donation.

Speaking of organ donation: Please share your thoughts on organ donation with each another. Should one of you need to make a decision about whether to donate the other partner's organs at their death, it really is helpful to know the deceased partner's wishes. If you want to be an organ donor, an easy way to identify yourself as one is a designation on your driver's license. Stating your preference on organ donation should also be spelled out in your Advance Directive.

A *Durable Health Care Power of Attorney* document allows you to appoint a trusted person to make medical decisions and to speak on your behalf should you become ill or incapacitated and not able to communicate your wishes.

A *Revocable Living Trust* is a document explaining how one's property will be distributed and managed during one's lifetime and after their death.

☑ If you currently have in place these three important documents, locate them and spend some time tonight reviewing the information. Have your wishes changed in regards to the preferences stated in your living will? Is the person you have appointed as Health Care Power of Attorney still the right choice? If you desire to make changes, a call to your estate attorney to revise the documents is in order.

☑ Develop a separate document for each family member of their medical history. Include a list of current doctors, their contact information, and the doctors' specialties. The medical histories should also mention current medical conditions, drug and other allergies, past surgeries, dates of those surgeries, and current medications (with specifics on dosages). Keep a copy of each medical history in your organization files.

An additional note about medical histories: If you are vacationing or on a business trip, having a copy of your family's medical histories will come in handy should you find yourself in an out-of-town hospital or emergency care center. If a trusted person is caring for your children while you are away and your child needs quick medical attention, you can confidently speak with medical staff, knowing the necessary information for your child is at your fingertips.

☑ Make copies of your family's medical insurance cards. If you have separate insurance cards for vision and dental, include those as well. Don't forget a copy of Medicare/ Medicaid, Medicare supplemental insurance, or Veterans Administration cards if you carry these insurances. Copy the front and back of each card. The back of these cards usually contains the contact information for the insurance company – vital to have in emergencies.

☑ Consider requesting from your dentist a copy of each family member's dental x-rays, especially if your family travels internationally. Add those to your organization files.

☑ This is a good time to discuss with each other your wish to be buried or cremated upon your death. Have you thought about funeral arrangements, such as the cemetery in which you wish to be buried, who is to officiate at your funeral service, favorite music to play at the service, the ten people who absolutely must know about your death?

Pre-planning your funerals can take the guesswork out of deciding the particulars of a funeral service and burial, leaving the living partner with more time to grieve with family and friends. Pre-planning does not necessarily mean pre-purchasing a cemetery plot and casket, although many couples in middle age do take advantage of making these selections while they are both still healthy and capable. Just a discussion of your preferences about the type of service you would like would help one another when those decisions need to be made at your deaths.

Many families use some of the proceeds from the life insurance policy on the deceased family member to pay for funeral and burial costs. This is especially helpful if the family prefers not to use their current cash, as these costs can run into the thousands of dollars. It just depends upon your personal situation and preference.

I once read an article about a group of friends (all female) who get together annually for a weekend to refresh their own obituaries! They talk about their achievements the past year, their highs and lows of daily living, and then set to work to construct – or tweak - the perfect obituary for themselves. Who better to write about yourself than *you*?

☑ Add to the file copies of military papers (yours and/or your partner's), along with specifics on any requests or plans for a military funeral. Families of eligible veterans can work with their funeral director to arrange for funeral honors. The funeral director will contact the appropriate Military Service to request a funeral honors detail. The family must specifically request a military honors service; simply notifying the funeral director the deceased was a military veteran or active service member is not sufficient. The original DD-214 (official military discharge document) must be obtained and presented in several arenas when a veteran dies. The original DD-214 provides proof the veteran served his/her country.

If and when the two of you have a discussion about these matters, jot down some notes and place them in the Medical tab of your organization files for future reference.

Results: By the end of this evening, the two of you should have:

☑ Planned to contact your attorney to create or revise your *Advance Directives, Durable Health Care Power of Attorney,* and your *Revocable Living Trust,* if needed.

☑ Made decisions pertaining to your wishes about medical and end-of-life care to include in the Advance Directives.

☑ Developed a medical history for each family member for your organization files.

A long night, but a productive one! Congratulations!

The Sixth Date Night

Your Contacts Organization Strategy

Be informed, not ignored.

Janet Bodnar, Author of *Money Smart Women*

What You'll Create Tonight:

Lists of all the important people in your lives. A list of all user IDs, passwords, and passcodes. Completion of the Contacts tab of your organization files.

What You'll Need:

This book, computer or notepad, pen, address book or contact list for both partners, a copier/scanner, your organization files.

A man passed away several months ago. His widow met with Peter Dunn, a financial advisor, and told him the following: "Peter, I have no idea what I'm doing. He handled everything. I haven't paid a bill in 40 years and don't even know where our accounts and bank accounts are. He had three different financial advisors, four different banks, and I don't know any of his passwords or PINs." *Courtesy of Peter Dunn (Pete the Planner).*[6]

Hello again. This date night will not discuss estate planning or financial matters, but I hope you are continuing to read books and articles on personal finance. We are working to build your financial savviness, so keep up the good work!

Tonight I would like the two of you to focus on everyone involved in your lives. If one (or both) of you becomes seriously ill, or is involved in an accident and is rushed to the hospital in a coma, will the other know whom to contact? If the answer to this question is "No," it is time to develop two contact lists.

☑ The first list consists of friends and family members you want to be contacted in case of emergencies. Develop a spreadsheet, hand-write the list, or create a group in your phone or computer contacts. The important thing is to note on the list the relationship of the contact to you and/or your partner. This is suggested for two reasons. First, if you have a trusted person making calls for you, they can handle the calls more easily if they know your relationship to the contact. Second, if you are trying to make calls, and you are in a stressful environment (dealing with an emergency at a hospital, trying to catch a flight at a bustling airport, etc.), you have one less thing to think about.

☑ The second list contains important people and companies you may need to contact in case of emergency. Here are some suggestions.

Name of Contact	Relationship	Phone number
Email address	Account Number	Additional Notes

Contacts to include:

- Employers and/or employees
- Neighbors
- Children's schools
- After-school activities (sports, music, etc.)
- Place of worship
- Membership clubs (book, fitness, social, etc.)
- Service Providers (tutors, lawn/landscape, housekeeper, etc.)
- Mortgage company
- Apartment leasing office
- Financial advisor
- Accountant
- Stock broker
- Attorney
- Volunteer locations
- Board memberships
- Utility companies (gas/electric, telephone, cable, water/sewer, etc.)

Once you have completed the lists, place copies into the Contacts tab of your organization files. If you have jointly decided to keep the contact lists in your phones or on a computer, please be sure you both know how to quickly access this information. Keeping a copy of these lists in the organization files is still a good option, especially if you hand off to a trusted friend or family member the chore of making calls.

☑ Develop a list of user IDs and passwords used by you, your partner, and your children. You would be surprised at the number of couples who do not know each other's passwords to open their cell phones, computers, and other electronic devices, as well as online passwords and user IDs. If you need to access your partner's email or social media accounts and don't have this information, gaining access is very difficult.

There are online password protection systems which securely store passwords in personal "vaults" or accounts. If you are computer savvy, these are very popular options with good security features.

☑ A list of home security system passcodes and storage facility access information should also be included in your organization file.

Results: By the end of this evening, the two of you should:

☑ Have begun or completed your lists of contacts.

☑ Have begun or completed your list of user IDs and passwords.

You've completed six of nine nights to financial empowerment and organization savviness. The next three date nights will be much easier. Keep up the good work!

The Seventh Date Night

Your Travel Documents Organization Strategy

No one realizes how beautiful it is to travel until he comes home and rests his head on his old, familiar pillow.

Lin Yutang

What You'll Create Tonight:

Completion of the Travel tab of your organization files.

What You'll Need:

This book, a copier/scanner, driver licenses, passports, visas, travel and airline cards, your organization files.

It's your seventh date night. Let's get into the travel mood. Prepare an exotic meal or keep it simple by picking up carry-out from your favorite ethnic restaurant. Put on some interesting music to enjoy.

Perhaps tonight's efforts will spur you to consider a second honeymoon…or a family getaway…or just a night watching *The Travel Channel*.

Please place copies of the following documents in the Travel tab of your organization file.

☑ Copies of passports and visas for you and your family. Check the expiration dates of the passports and visas; if they expire within six months, make a calendar reminder to renew. Several countries will not accept a U.S. passport if it expires fewer than six months from the date of travel.

☑ Copies of driver licenses for you and your family. Check the expiration of the licenses to see if you have a renewal coming up soon.

☑ Copies of domestic and international travel cards for you and your family, if you have them.

☑ Copies of airline mileage or travel membership cards for you and your family, if you have them.

Results: By the end of this evening, the two of you should have:

☑ Copied all your travel documents in your organization files.

☑ Determined if your passports and/or visas need renewal.

☑ Scheduled a calendar reminder to renew your driver licenses if they are coming up for renewal.

Congratulations - you are becoming an organization whiz! Two date nights to go.

The Eighth Date Night

Your Business Documents Organization Strategy

To be prepared is half the victory.

Miguel De Cervantes, Spanish novelist

What You'll Create Tonight:

Completion of the Business tab of your organization files.

What You'll Need:

Copier/scanner, your organization files, business partnership agreements, continuation plans, business contacts, bank information, business charge cards, outside advisor contact information.

$\mathcal{D}$ on't own a business? You're not allowed to skip this date night! Your assignment instead is to go online to read financial blogs or articles. Or, if you have borrowed or purchased books on financial matters, read aloud to one another and discuss a few topics of interest. Refer to the Bibliography at the end of this book for many good books to consider.

If you and/or your partner do own a business, it is important to include, in the Business tab of your organization file, some information pertinent to your business:

☑ A copy of *Partnership Agreements* (business or personal) and the contact information for the other partners in the business.

☑ A copy of any business contracts currently in place.

☑ Include a copy of the business continuation plan that may activate with the death of the owner or partner.

☑ Make a copy of the *Declarations Page* of any business insurance you carry, such as Workers' Compensation, Liability, Errors and Omissions, etc.

☑ A copy of any loans carried by the business.

☑ A list of bank accounts, type of account, and account numbers owned by the business, including contact information for the bank. Don't forget user ID and passwords if you bank online for your business. Include a note as to the owners and authorized users of these accounts.

☑ If there are credit or debit cards owned by the business, include a copy of the cards (front and back) in your organization file.

☑ Insert into the file a list of business contacts, such as clients, suppliers, employees, bankers, attorneys, and insurance carriers.

Results: By the end of this evening, the two of you should have:

☑ (If you own a business) Reviewed the language of the business continuation plan and partnership agreements to be sure all information is current.

☑ If your assignment tonight was to read up on financial information, continue this practice at least monthly. Don't skip over reading the financial articles in your local newspaper or listening to financial news on the television or radio. All are good sources of up-to-the-minute knowledge you can use for your benefit.

One more date night to go. You're nearly there!

The Ninth Date Night

Your Strategy to Capture Everything Else

Now is the time for you to attend to your own financial self-defense.

June Mays, Author of *Women's Guide to Financial Self-Defense*

What You'll Create Tonight:

Completion of the Other tab of your organization files.

What You'll Need:

This book, a copier/scanner, your organization files, information on subscriptions, membership/volunteer efforts, notes on home information, notes or paperwork on collections (art, jewelry, etc.) you own.

It's your ninth date night. You have both worked hard on this project, so make this evening extra-special. Put on your favorite music, dine on great food, share an intimate conversation. You both deserve it!

Your organization files are not yet complete. Take a few moments and think about anything else you should include in the files under the Other tab. Here are few suggestions.

- ☑ A note about memberships owned by you and/or your partner and other family members, both online and other. Include in your organization files a copy of any member cards you have.

- ☑ A list of subscriptions, both digital and print.

- ☑ A list of important home information (water shut-off instructions, alarm codes, location of spare keys, etc.).

- ☑ Speaking of spare keys, consider keeping a set in one of your organization files.

- ☑ If you have collectibles, jewelry, fine arts, or other valuables, a list of these and their location(s). If these items will be bequeathed in your estate planning, add a note about the recipients and the item(s) they are to receive.

- ☑ Add a note about any outstanding loans you have made to others. Include the amount of the loan, the terms, and the contact information for the borrower.

- ☑ If you have loaned a treasured item to someone, such as a book or piece of jewelry, include a note about the item, the date of the loan, and the contact information for the person who borrowed the item.

Results: By the end of this evening:

Your organization files should now contain copies or originals of the most important documents of your lives. You are ready for any emergency. Remind yourselves to review the contents at least once a year.

Remember to keep all your original documents secured safely, whether in a safe deposit box, home safe, or other option. Your emergency documents file, containing copies of all the originals, should also be safely stored, but quickly accessible.

Great job!

Final Thoughts

$\mathcal{A}$nd there you have it. Through a series of nine date nights, you have increased your financial wisdom, improved your financial vocabulary, and developed very useful files of the most important documents you need in case of emergencies. I officially proclaim you Co-CFOs. Congratulations!

If you have adult children, talk to them about your organization files, where they are located, and the reasons why you developed this tool. They might feel a file of their own would be a good strategy for their families.

If you have older parents and feel they could benefit from developing their own organization files, show them yours and explain how the process can help them keep track of their paperwork. Prompt them to review their current documents.

As one of the first points of contact in case of an emergency, notify your financial advisor or accountant about your organization files.

Review and update your information at least annually. This will be your Anniversary Date Night, so circle one more date about a year from now to keep the process going.

Continue to study, prepare, and participate in your financial lives! Keep working to improve your financial vocabulary and your knowledge of financial concepts and strategies. The nine date nights are just the beginning of your journey to financial empowerment. In time, your confidence and clarity on all things financial will be a tremendous benefit to you and to your family.

All the best to you!

Notes

1   Centers for Disease Control National Vital Statistics Program, 2010

2   *Conscious Company Magazine*, Summer, 2015 Issue 3

3   Siegel, Cary, *Why Didn't They Teach Me This In School? 99 Personal Money Management Principles to Live By*, Simple Strategic Solutions LLC, 2015.

4   Holsapple, Scott, The Mutual Fund Store, cited in the article "7 Tips for Women about to Retire," Rodney Brooks on Retirement, USA Today/Indianapolis Star, 7/6/2014 (print).

5   Hannon, Kerry, *Suddenly Single: Money Skills for Divorcees and Widows*, John Wiley & Sons, 1998.

6   "Keep Your Family in the Financial Loop," Peter Dunn (Pete the Planner), *Indianapolis Star*, 2/16/14 (print).

Bibliography

Yes, you've just committed nine nights to expanding your financial wisdom. So why stop now? Put your new-found financial knowledge and strategies to good use, and keep reading! Here are some recommendations.

Online Articles and Websites

Women Can Build Their Own Golden Nest Egg, by Rodney Brooks, *USA Today,* November 14, 2013.

7 Tip$ for Women About to Retire, by Rodney Brooks, *USA Today,* July 6, 2014.

7 Big Mistakes Couples Make in Retirement, by Rodney Brooks, *USA Today,* April 13, 2014.

Nice Girls Talk About Estate Planning by Deborah L. Jacobs, Forbes online article.

The Critical Importance of Estate Planning for Women by Michael Lichterman, Esq., August 28, 2011, online article.

The Importance of Estate Planning for Women, Bingham Greenebaum Doll, August 1, 2009, online article.

10 Estate Planning Tips for Women by Angie Mohr, Investopedia.com, July 26, 2012, online article.

The Wealth Transfer, Conscious Company Magazine, Summer 2015 Issue 3 (print).

6 Ways a Financial Planner Can Charge Fees by Dana Anspach, http://moneyover55.about.com, online article.

6 Things to Do Before Your Spouse Dies by Barbara Stanny, www.forbes.com, online article.

Why You Shouldn't Let Your Partner Do The Books by Glenn Curtis, www.Investopedia.com, online article.

A To-Do List for the Surviving Spouse by Susan B. Garland, www.Kiplinger.com, online article. Good list of what widows and widowers need to do in the months following their spouse's death. Also good information to have on hand *before* the death of a spouse.

Money Mistakes Women Make – 3 Tips for Fixing Financial Blunders by Laurie Pawlik-Kienlen, www.theadventurouswriter.com/blog/, online article.

Keep Your Family in the Financial Loop, Peter Dunn (Pete the Planner), Indianapolis Star, 2/16/14 (print).

Peter Dunn's website, www.petetheplanner.com, is full of ideas, information, resources, *and* you can subscribe to a free newsletter. Peter writes with humor, intelligence, and experience.

http://personal-finance.thefuntimesguide.com is an online site with many articles on personal finance.

http://www.financialized.com has good articles and information on personal and corporate finance issues.

http://www.practicalmoneyskills.com is another online site with apps, games and other information for the entire family.

http://kidmoney.about.com provides a list of games about money management for children.

http.//www.edutopia.org has an article by Andrew Miller with a list of recommended games to teach financial literacy.

Printed Books

Estate Planning Basics by Denis Clifford, NOLO Law for All, 2013.

The Wall Street Journal Complete Estate-Planning Guidebook by Rachel Emma Silverman, Dow Jones & Company, 2011.

Estate Planning for Blended Families by Richard E. Barnes, NOLO, 2009.

Estate Planning: A Road Map for Beginners by Susan G. Parker, Esq. and Maria B. Whealan, Esq., Parker Press, Inc., 2014.

Financial Terms Dictionary: Terminology Plain and Simple Explained by Thomas Herold and Wesley David Crowder, Self-Published/Evolving Wealth, LLC, 2014.

Women's Guide to Financial Self-Defense by June Mays, Warner Books, 1997.

Suddenly Single: Money Skills for Divorcees and Widows by Kerry Hannon, John Wiley & Sons, 1998. Very thorough explanations of how to wend your way through financial thickets -- before and after divorce or widowhood.

Prince Charming Isn't Coming: How Women Get Smart About Money, by Barbara Stanny, Penguin Books, 1999.

Money Smart Women, by Janet Bodnar, Kaplan Publishing, 2006. Chapter 4 of this book shows how women can and should avoid being a "silent partner" when it comes to finances in a marriage.

Women & Money: Owning the Power to Control Your Destiny, by Suze Orman, Spiegel & Grau, 2010.

Why Didn't They Teach Me This In School? 99 Personal Money Management Principles to Live By, by Cary Siegel, Simple Strategic Solutions LLC, 2015. Great book to give to your teenagers and young adults. It's like a condensed course in personal financial management, easy to understand and very topical to young people.

What Every Woman Should Know About Her Husband's Money, by Shelby White, iUniverse.com, 2000. Originally published in 1995 and re-issued in 2000, but still very on-point in terms of the roles men and women fall into with regard to money management.

Moving Forward on Your Own: A Financial Guidebook for Widows, by Kathleen M. Rehl, PhD., CFP©, Rehl Financial Advisors, 2010. Pages 24-27 talks about organizing information, whom to contact, and what financial information to review.

How to Say It to Seniors: Closing the Communication Gap with Our Elders, by David Solie, M.S., P.A., Penguin Publishing Group, 2004. Why include this book in the bibliography? If you plan to have a discussion with your aging parents about the need for their own organization file or to encourage your mother to become more comfortable with talking about finances (and I hope you do), this book has terrific information on communicating successfully with older folks.

Glossary of Financial Terminology

It's a great idea to familiarize yourself with some of the basic terminology and the strategies behind the use of estate planning, personal finance and investment tools. This short list of terms is just the tip of the iceberg, but it's a good start. These websites provide solid definitions and explanations of the terminology:

http://www.estateplanning.com/Estate-Planning-Glossary/

https://www.fidelity.com/glossary/estate-planning-inheritance

http://www.investopedia.com/dictionary/

401(k) plan: A defined contribution plan offered by a company to its eligible employees. Allows employees to set aside tax-deferred income for retirement purposes. In some cases, employers will match the contribution at a certain percentage. There are several types of 401(k) plans (SIMPLE, Roth, individual) depending upon the type of company.

403(b) plan: Retirement plan, similar to a 401(k), but is offered by non-profit organizations.

Adjusted Gross Income (AGI): Also referred to as net income. Calculated by subtracting allowable deductions, such as alimony, medical expenses, etc., from gross income.

Advance Directive: An Advance Directive, also called a living will, spells out your preferences for medical care. This includes whether you choose to receive medical care; pain relief methods; end-of-life directions on providing or withholding nutrition and resuscitation; and your preferences on organ donation.

Alimony: Payments made to a former spouse under a divorce or separation agreement. Alimony is taxable income for the receiver, and a deductible expense for the payer.

Annuity: A type of investment where a fixed amount of money is paid to the person establishing the annuity (the annuitant) for a fixed period of time.

Appraisal: The process of placing a value on an asset or property.

Appreciation: The increase in value of an asset or property.

Asset: Anything of monetary value owned by a person.

Basis: How much one pays for an asset, such as investments or a home. Basis can be increased by capital improvements (such as a home renovation) or decreased by items such as depreciation, and is used to compute taxable gain on the sale or exchange of the property.

Beneficiary, Contingent: The person or persons named to receive distributions (cash, stocks and bonds, jewelry or fine arts are examples) from a trust, a will, or a life insurance policy in the event the primary beneficiaries are unable to receive the distributions. For example, if the primary beneficiary chooses not to receive the assets, or dies before taking ownership of the assets, the contingent beneficiary would then receive the assets.

Beneficiary, Primary: The person or persons named to receive distributions (cash, stocks and bonds, jewelry or fine arts are examples) from a trust, a will, or a life insurance policy.

Bequest: The gift of an asset or property under the terms of a will.

Bond: A debt investment where an investor loans money to an entity, which borrows the funds for a defined period of time at a fixed or variable interest rate. Used by corporations and municipalities to raise money and finance projects and activities.

Capital Gains and Losses: Increase or decrease in the value of a capital asset. The gain is not realized until the asset is sold. Short term gains or losses are one year or less; long term gains and losses refer to assets held more than one year.

Cash Flow: The amount of money received (income, interest and dividends, child support, alimony, etc.) measured against the amount of money spent (mortgage, rent, utilities, credit card payments, etc.).

Certified Copy: A copy of a primary document, containing an endorsement or certification, which it is a true copy of the primary document.

Certified Financial Planner (CFP©): A financial professional who is certified by the Certified Financial Planner Board of Standards, Inc. A candidate for the CFP designation must have extensive experience in this field, and is required to take exams and annual continuing education programs in financial planning, taxes, insurance, estate planning, and retirement.

Chartered Life Underwriter (CLU): Designation for financial professionals who have completed coursework in life insurance and estate planning.

Child Support: Monetary payments, usually made by a noncustodial parent to the parent who has custody of the child/children. Child support is not tax deductible by the payer, and is tax-free to the recipient. Child support is paid only until the child reaches the age of majority.

Codicil: A separate document serving as an addendum to a will. Used to keep a will current and up to date without rewriting the entire will.

Common Stock: A security representing ownership in a corporation. Holders of common stock can exercise control by electing a board of directors and voting on corporate policy.

Credit Report: Prepared by a credit bureau (Equifax, Trans Union and Experian are the three largest bureaus in the United States). A credit report details a person's payment history and ability to repay debts. Credit reports are used by lenders to assess a loan applicant's credit worthiness.

Credit Score: A numeric expression of one's ability to repay debts. The score – a number between 300 and 850 - uses a person's past credit and payment history. The higher the score, the better one's credit history and one's ability to negotiate interest rates and terms for future loans.

Decedent: A deceased person.

Depreciation: The decrease in value of an asset or property.

Disability Insurance, Short-term and Long-term: An insurance policy paying benefits in the event the policyholder becomes unable to work.

Dividend, Cash: Paid to shareholders in the form of cash, usually from the corporation's earnings or accumulated profits, and are paid on a per-share basis. Dividends are considered taxable income to the recipients.

Dividend, Stock: Dividend payment made in the form of additional shares rather than cash.

Durable Health Care Power of Attorney: Document allowing you to appoint a trusted person to make medical decisions and to speak on your behalf should you become ill and unable to communicate your wishes specified in the Advance Directive.

Estate Tax: Tax levied by the state or the federal government on the assets of a deceased person. The estate is obligated to pay the estate tax.

Executor/Executrix: A person s named to administer the estate of a deceased person; i.e., to carry out the instructions and wishes of the deceased. Executrix is the feminine version of Executor.

General Durable Power of Attorney: A legal document where one person (the principal) gives another (the agent) authorization to act for the principal in some agreed upon manner.

Grantor: A person who creates a trust.

Guardian: A person who is given the legal responsibility to care for a minor child or for an adult who is not capable of self-care.

Health Care Representative: A person who has been named a medical power of attorney to make medical decisions on behalf of someone else.

Hedge Fund: Similar to mutual funds, hedge funds are a pooled investment that can participate in a variety of securities (equities, bonds, options, etc.). Hedge funds have a different fee structure than mutual funds, and can be a riskier investment.

Incapacity: The condition of a person who is unable to manage his or her affairs due to mental or physical impairment.

Individual Retirement Account (IRA): A retirement account permitting the account holder to set aside money each year, with earnings tax-deferred until withdrawals begin.

Intestate: Dying without a valid will.

Life Insurance: An investment providing a cash distribution (death benefit) upon the policy owner's death to named beneficiaries. Generally used to help make up for income lost due to the death of the policy holder. Several types of life insurance are available (whole life, universal life, variable life, etc.)

Living Trust: See Trust, Living.

Living Will: See Advance Directive.

Long-term Care Insurance: Insurance policy paying for extended medical care in the event the policyholder becomes unable to care for her/himself for an extended period of time.

Mutual Fund: Investment vehicle comprised of a pool of funds to invest in securities.

Net Worth: The amount by which one's assets exceed one's liabilities.

Partnership Agreement: A written document that details the duties and responsibilities of the partners, the nature of the partnership, the partners' profit sharing ratio, etc.

Personal Financial Statement: A report of one's assets, liabilities, and resulting net worth.

Personal Representative: A person given the authority to make decisions on behalf of someone. Also is another name for the executor or administrator of the estate of a deceased person.

Preferred Stock: Ownership in a corporation with a higher claim on assets and earnings than common stock. Generally has a dividend which must be paid before common stock dividends.

Prenuptial Agreement: A contract created, before becoming married, which outlines the terms and conditions for dividing financial assets and property, and discusses responsibilities if the marriage ends.

Present Value: Typically defined as the amount of money needed today to meet a future expense, given an assumed rate of return.

Probate: A court proceeding to determine the validity of a will. The oversight of the procedure by which the assets of a decedent are administered under the provisions of a will.

Roth IRA: An individual retirement plan similar to a traditional IRA, but contributions are not tax deductible and qualified distributions are tax free.

Tax-deferred Investment: Where pre-tax dollars are invested. Taxes are paid when the investments are sold. Used extensively for retirement planning. The presumption is, when the investments are sold, the owner will be in a lower tax bracket than when the investment was first made.

Time Value of Money: A basic concept in finance stating money available at the present time is worth more than the same amount in the future due to its potential earing capacity. In other words, if money can earn interest, it is worth more the sooner it is received.

Trust, Irrevocable: A trust whose provisions cannot be altered or canceled by the grantor of the trust without the beneficiary's permission.

Trust, Living: Estate planning tool allowing the control of assets before and after death.

Trust, Revocable: A trust where provisions can be altered or canceled by the grantor of the trust.

Trustee: A person or firm holding or administering property or assets for the benefit of a third party. As the name implies, trustees are trusted to make decisions in the beneficiary's best interest.

Umbrella Insurance: Additional liability coverage providing another layer of security to those at risk for being sued for damages to other people's property or injuries caused to others in an accident. An umbrella policy is helpful when the insurance owner is sued and the dollar limit of the original policy is exhausted.

Will: A signed, written legal document where a person (the testator) names one or more persons to manage his/her estate and provides for the distribution of assets and property at the death of the will's writer.

Appendix A

What Would Happen if One of Us Dies?

*Because when the time comes, your loved one needs a chance to grieve.
And if they're trying to hack the family computer for information, then
the grieving gets delayed.*

Peter Dunn, from the print article
"Keep Your Family in the Financial Loop"[6]

A loving gesture you can make to each other is to prepare yourselves now in the event one of you passes away. You have prepared your estate planning and medical emergency care documents. You have developed your organization files. And now I offer a to-do list for the surviving partner. This checklist should help you through a most difficult episode in your life with more confidence and clarity.

What Do I Do?

First, you will need to contact many people. It may be helpful for you to enlist a trusted friend or family member to assist you with making these calls.

☑ Your partner's employer (and yours, to let them know you will be unavailable for a period of time).

☑ Funeral home/cemetery. If the deceased partner requested a military honors service, be sure to let the funeral director know so arrangements can be made, including arranging for a flag to drape on the casket. The original DD-214 (official military discharge document) must be obtained and presented in several arenas when a veteran dies. The DD-214 form provides proof the veteran served his/her country.

☑ Your family's minister or member of the clergy, to arrange for a religious service, if one is desired.

☑ Family members, friends and neighbors.

☑ Your financial advisor. He/she will be a terrific resource for you and your family during this time.

☑ Your accountant will also be able to assist you. An early call to your CPA will help him/her in preparing any necessary tax documentation. The CPA can also make a note for the timeline to file the estate tax return (due nine months after death).

☑ Your children's schools and outside activities.

All these contacts will already be in your organization files.

Next, you will need to plan the funeral. Decisions to be made, and the related costs to consider, include:

☑ A casket for burial or an urn for cremation.

☑ The funeral service.

☑ Flowers/memorials.

☑ A dinner, open house, or other gathering for the mourners.

☑ A cemetery plot and headstone.

☑ Writing and submitting an obituary to the local newspaper.

If the two of you make these decisions ahead of time, this process is easier. A note in your organization files will be ready for you when working through these decisions.

☑ Contact the Health Department to request 10-15 *certified copies* of the death certificate at no charge. The funeral director can order these for you, but there will be a cost for the service. You will need several certified copies of the death certificate to submit when claiming benefits, renaming assets, closing accounts, etc. Having the copies ahead of time will save you an extra step down the road.

After the service, give yourself and your family some time to grieve before beginning the next phase – filing for benefits. Thanks to your organization files, you will have all this information immediately available to you.

☑ Contact your life insurance agent to begin the process of collecting benefits. These funds will help with funeral costs, so it's a good idea to contact the agent within a week or two of your partner's passing.

☑ If you can collect Social Security benefits, submit a claim with the Social Security Administration. As of the writing of this book, Social Security also provides $225 to the surviving partner as a death benefit.

☑ If your partner was active in the military or a veteran, contact the Veterans Administration to inquire about benefits for your family.

☑ If your family had health insurance coverage through your deceased partner's plan, check to see how long coverage continues.

☑ If your partner had disability or long-term care insurance coverage, now is the time to cancel those policies. A call to the insurance company, or to your life insurance agent, will take care of this.

☑ Discuss with your financial advisor the process of putting your deceased partner's assets into your name, or rolling over your partner's IRA assets into your IRA account.

☑ Contact the human resources department of your partner's employer to inquire about unpaid salary, vacation and other benefits you may be entitled to.

☑ Contact your insurance agent. Your auto insurance policy premium may be reduced with one less driver on your policy.

☑ Then begin the process of assessing your cash flow needs. Don't forget to continue paying bills as they come due, if the checking/savings accounts are jointly owned. If the accounts are solely owned by your deceased partner, they will become part of your partner's estate and will be paid from the assets of the estate.

☑ The mortgage, rent, car loan, credit card statements and other expenses (again, if jointly owned) should be paid on time. Although this will be a very difficult time for you, it is important to keep your *credit score* and credit rating at a good level. Schedule regular bill paying dates to keep everything current.

☑ When you feel ready, arrange to meet with your financial advisor and your accountant to discuss next steps in the estate settlement and tax filing process. The estate tax return must be filed nine months after death.

Appendix B

Sources for Organization Tools

www.Amazon.com sells many variations of good-quality accordion folders with a flap cover at reasonable prices. Your local office supply store will have additional options to consider.

Cloud-based storage options: PC Magazine online (www.pcmag.com) offers recommendations on the top products for backup and document storage.

My website, www.organizedsolutionsllc.net, provides information on "Get Us Organized!" sessions I offer.

For the Record: A Personal Facts & Document Organizer, Ricky Sue Pagano, Five Star Publications, 2007. Print

Get It Together: Organize Your Records So Your Family Won't Have To, Melanie Cullen with Shae Irving, J.D., NOLO Law for All, 2014.

LifeSafe Personal and Home Organizer by Michelle Burton, www.lifesafe.com

Index

About the Author

$\mathcal{L}$aurie Teal has spent the past 25 years successfully working with clients in administration, project management, and home/office/ financial organization. As a wife and mother, she has deftly managed her family's financial and organizational needs.

She now shares this experience and knowledge to encourage partners to actively participate in and organize their financial lives.

45026250R00049

Made in the USA
San Bernardino, CA
30 January 2017